Stoicism and Mental Health

A Path to Inner Peace

Table of Contents

Chapter 1. Introduction

Dive into a journey of self-transformation with our Special Report: "Stoicism and Mental Health: A Path to Inner Peace". This enlightening guide offers a soothing balm to the troubled minds of our times. Interweaving the timeless wisdom of ancient Stoic philosophy with modern mental health practices, this guide is designed to lead you on a path towards inner peace and stability, irrespective of the turmoil outside. Let's unravel the secrets hidden in the serene world of stoicism together to rebuild, rejuvenate, and restore your mental prowess. A life of tranquility is just a page away - begin your voyage towards a more balanced, more resilient you today. By purchasing this special report, you're not just buying a document, you're investing in a brighter, more tranquil future!

Chapter 2. Unveiling Stoicism: An Introduction

The fabric of human life has experienced incessant changes since the dawn of time. In the maelthstrom of these shifts, human civilization has always searched for an anchor- a philosophical pier that would provide stability amidst the volatile waves of existence. One such philosophy that has emerged powerful and useful is Stoicism. Originating from the bustling plazas of ancient Greece, Stoicism, a school of Hellenistic philosophy, has imparted profound wisdom on the human condition and how best to navigate it.

2.1. A dive into the Origin of Stoicism

Stoicism was founded in Athens, Greece by Zeno of Citium in the early 3rd century BC. Its teachings brushed off the concepts of abstract metaphysics and grand narratives in favor of practical wisdom, personal virtue, and moral action.

The story unfolds when Zeno, a successful merchant, found himself shipwrecked with his cargo lost at sea. This incident led Zeno to the realization that external events are beyond our control and that tranquility and peace should come from how we accept and respond to them. This sudden epiphany prompted Zeno to lay the foundation for Stoicism.

The philosophy had rapidly burgeoned, with noteworthy advocates such as Seneca, Epictetus, and Emperor Marcus Aurelius contributing to the steady maturation of Stoicism. Each played a pivotal role, piecing together the jigsaw puzzle of Stoicism in their unique ways.

2.2. Stoicism's Core Beliefs

Stoicism's foundation is built upon the premise of living a life consistent with nature, accepting the outcome of events outside of our control, and focusing predominantly on what we can indeed change - our perception and reactions.

Stoic philosophy hones in on four core virtues: Wisdom, Courage, Justice, and Temperance. Each of these cardinal virtues offers essential guidance in different areas of life. Wisdom equates not to the learning of more facts but rather the ability to make sound judgments. Courage here is moral courage, the ability to take right action despite fear. Justice refers to the ethical consideration of others in all our actions, while Temperance is the art of self-restraint.

Stoicism fervently advocates the dichotomy of control. It encourages identifying those facets of life that are within our grasp and those that aren't. This simple yet profound notion lets us conserve our energies on aspects we can change, leaving us better placed to cope with trials and tribulations that life presents.

2.3. Practical Applications of Stoicism in Daily Life

Stoicism is not merely an abstract theoretical field of study. It is a praxis—an active application and exercise of philosophy in daily life. In modern times, its teachings can be applied to a wide array of situations, including mental health, business decisions, relationship issues, coping with negative emotions, and the constant pursuit of success.

Consider negative emotions, for instance, like anger, grief, disappointment, or anxiety - these are inevitable human experiences. The Stoic approach would encourage us to accept the emotion but to select a rational and manageable response. Your boss has upset you not because of his actions or words, rather by your interpretation of them, a classic Stoic thought.

Similarly, in business decisions or personal situations, Stoicism's core principle of understanding what is within our control could help alleviate unnecessary stress. For example, in preparing for a job interview, you can make sure your skills are sharp, your dress is suitable, and you arrive on time. However, whether you get the job or not is outside of your control, a decision that lies with the interviewer.

2.4. Stoicism and Mental Health

One of the resounding echoes of Stoicism in the modern world is its applicability in the field of mental health. The Stoic philosophy harmonizes remarkably well with various therapeutic practices such as Cognitive Behavioral Therapy (CBT). It provides tools to reframe adverse situations and realize that our reaction to a situation carries more weight than the situation itself.

CBT and Stoicism share common ground in enumerating that a significant part of emotional turmoil arises from irrational beliefs or cognitive distortions. Recognizing and changing these irrational thoughts can significantly alter emotional and behavioral outcomes.

Some techniques that transcend from Stoic philosophy into mental health practices are negative visualization (envisioning worse scenarios to appreciate the present), practicing misfortune (voluntarily subjecting oneself to uncomfortable situations to grow resilience), and voluntary discomfort to cultivate fortitude.

Stoicism doesn't sell a magical cure but offers a shift in perspective. It nudges us to be more accepting and understanding, teaching us to not crumble when met with adversity but to stand tall and resilient.

2.5. The Everlasting Relevance of Stoicism

Through centuries of rapid changes and unparalleled human advancements, Stoicism remains as relevant as ever. The simplicity of its core tenets - the control dichotomy, being in harmony with nature, refining our responses - chimes with the needs of the modern world.

Whether you're a teenager navigating the thorny path of adolescence, a stressed professional wrestling your work-life balance, or a senior citizen making sense of the autumn years, Stoicism has something to offer. It's a philosophy that is timeless in its insights and universal in its appeal.

We've merely skimmed the surface of this profound philosophy, presented a glimpse of the outline. As we delve further into the upcoming sections, we will explore the nitty-gritty of Stoic principles, their application, and how Stoicism can pave the path towards attaining inner peace.

Chapter 3. Underpinnings of Stoicism and its Core Principles

Stoicism was born in Athens around 300 BC at a time when philosophers pursued queries about existence, the true nature of reality, virtue and ethics. The stoic philosophy was developed by the thought leader Zeno of Citium. Over centuries, themes of Stoicism have evolved, branching into cohesive principles that continue to navigate our human existence.

3.1. Development of Stoic Philosophy

The foundational beliefs of Stoic philosophy are still firmly grounded in its ancient roots. Zeno, initially inspired by Socratic thought, found the core of his approach in the principle of attaining tranquility through the understanding of our emotions and control of our responses. However, Zeno wasn't the last philosopher to contribute to the school of Stoicism. Other philosophers such as Cleanthes, Chrysippus, Seneca, Epictetus, and Marcus Aurelius amplified Stoicism, placing emphasis on Ethic, Logic, and Physics that eventually shaped the discipline.

3.1.1. Early Stoa

Under the guidance of Zeno, Cleanthes, and Chrysippus, the early Stoa began to form the fundamental principles of Stoic philosophy. It detached from metaphysical speculations, concentrating more on achieving eudaimonia - the highest human good, which in Stoic philosophy, is attained through virtue. Chrysippus with his logical argumentation and coherent presentation of Stoicism bolstered its popularity.

3.1.2. Middle Stoa

Transitioning into the Middle Stoa during the 1st century BC, Stoic philosophy was spread to Rome by philosophers such as Panaetius and Posidonius. They brought much needed adaptability, bridging the gap between high philosophy and everyday life, making the philosophy more accessible to the Roman audience.

3.1.3. Late Stoa

The late Stoa is epitomized by three intellectuals: Seneca, Epictetus, and Emperor Marcus Aurelius. Their writings are the psychological backbone of Stoicism, deeply analyzing the self, passions, and emotions. Their works are still popular today due to their powerfully poetic language and timelessly practical advice.

3.2. Acceptance and Action

One salient facet of Stoicism is the distinction between what's within our control (such as our actions and thoughts) and what's not (such as the actions of others, the weather, or death). Navigating this distinction is the key to emotional resilience and satisfaction, encouraging proactive behavior while fostering acceptance of what we can't change.

3.3. Virtue: The Highest Good

Stoicism places virtue at the peak of human excellence. Core virtues include wisdom (insight into the nature of things), justice (treat everyone fairly), courage (perseverance and bravery), and temperance (moderation and self-control). According to Stoics, one could lead a blessed life by embracing and practicing these virtues.

3.4. Living According to Nature

Often misunderstood, Stoics' advice to "live according to nature" doesn't advocate a simplistic return to a naturalistic lifestyle. Instead, it means living in harmony with the universe's rational and social nature. This lived philosophy implies understanding our place in the universal scheme and performing our roles dutifully and virtuously.

3.5. Stoic Dichotomy of Control

Perhaps one of the most beneficial teachings of Stoicism is the 'Dichotomy of Control'. Stoics affirm that understanding the division between what we can and can't control can guide us towards peace. When we focus on what's in our control, such as our attitudes, behaviours, and responses, we can navigate life with equanimity.

3.6. Socratic Influence

Stoicism's roots lie in Socratic philosophy, primarily in the focus on virtue and ethics. Socratic intellectualism strikes a chord with Stoic principles due to the shared belief that knowledge can lead to virtue and ignorance to vice. The Socratic method of inquiry has deeply influenced Stoic techniques of self-examination.

3.7. Stoicism and Emotion

Stoics don't advocate devoiding oneself of emotions but underpin the regulation and understanding of excessive pathological emotions (passions). According to Stoicism, the mind shouldn't be controlled by reckless passions but steered by reasoned judgement.

The Stoic journey is characterized by daily practice, self-reflection, and incremental progress. It's not about achieving a destination, but about embracing the path to inner tranquility, no matter the outward circumstances. The guiding principles of Stoicism offer a robust framework to lead a life of purpose, virtue, and tranquility in this fast-paced modern world. It does so by harmonizing our existence with the broader cosmos, leading us to understanding, acceptance and inner peace.

Chapter 4. Stoicism and Emotional Resilience

From the onset, one might question the relevance of stoicism, an ancient philosophical doctrine, in the face of modern psychological difficulties and challenges. However, the principles of stoicism are remarkably applicable in the cultivation and enhancement of emotional resilience. This chapter will dig deep into this relation, unravelling the profound potency of stoicism for contemporary mental health and providing practical guidance to integrate its wisdom into daily life.

4.1. The Essence of Stoicism

Stoicism was an influential philosophy of the Hellenistic period and later in Rome, propounded by noteworthy figures such as Seneca, Marcus Aurelius, and Epictetus. Central to stoic philosophy is the acceptance of the world as it is and viewing difficulties as ingredients of life rather than exceptions to it. Stoicism asserts that we don't have control over external events but, importantly, we have absolute control over our internal world - our reactions, perceptions, and judgments. This is at the core of emotional resilience, the ability to adapt and recover from stressors, adversities, trauma or hardship.

4.2. Stoicism and Emotional Resilience: A Natural Correlation

Emotional resilience is often defined as our capacity to bounce back or recover from stressful or challenging situations. In a stoic lens, it is intrinsically linked to the ability to control the inner narrative. When we can effectively control how we perceive, interpret, and react to events, we are simultaneously fostering emotional resilience. Stoics regard emotional turbulence as a concoction of our judgments and reactions to events rather than the events themselves. This is not to deny the existence of devastating external circumstances but rather to bring into focus the enormous power we have over our emotional responses.

4.3. Dealing with Pain and Suffering

Ancient Stoics had a unique perspective on pain and suffering altogether. They saw it not as events to be avoided at all costs, but merely as a part of human existence. Pain was a teacher, and suffering was a test of character. Misfortune was an opportunity to apply and demonstrate virtue. Emotional resilience, similarly, reinforces the ability to confront pain and suffering, learning from the experience and growing stronger as a result.

Marcus Aurelius, a prominent Stoic philosopher, penned in his 'Meditations', "The impediment to action advances action. What stands in the way becomes the way." This statement beautifully encapsulates the crux of resilience. It calls upon us to shift our paradigm of adversities, viewing them as stepping stones towards emotional growth and strength.

4.4. Techniques for Intensifying Emotional Resilience

Stoicism offers several hands-on strategies that can enhance emotional resilience. A key practice known as 'negative visualization' involves routinely contemplating worst-case scenarios to lessen the dread surrounding potential misfortunes and strengthen our emotional acceptance of life's challenges. The premeditation of adversity thus is a reminder of the impermanent nature of material comforts, fostering reliance on one's virtues and inner strengths.

Another powerful technique is 'voluntary discomfort', where one deliberately exposes oneself to uncomfortable situations. This voluntary self-exposure to hardship cultivates robustness, reduces fear, and prepares the individual for potential adversities.

4.5. The Modern Appeal of Stoicism

The surged interest in stoicism in the 21st century isn't accidental. Emotional resilience, a quality highly sought after in our challenging and fast-paced modern world, is deeply rooted in the principles of stoic philosophy. The recent convergence of stoicism and cognitive behavioral therapy (CBT), a modern psychological treatment, is a testament to the enduring relevance and effectiveness of stoic philosophy. CBT borrows heavily from stoicism in its emphasis on controlling one's responses to external stimuli to enhance mental health.

Emotional resilience is a learned skill. It is not static, but an ever-evolving, nurturing process. The bridge between the ancient wisdom of stoicism and modern mental health offers an extraordinary pathway for cultivating emotional resilience. As Seneca profoundly stated, "We suffer more in imagination than in reality", highlighting our emotional resilience truly lies in our hands. By harnessing the wisdom of stoic philosophy, we can indeed take command of our minds and lead a mentally healthier, more tranquil life.

Chapter 5. Mental Health: The Modern Context

In a world where stress, anxiety, and disturbances have become the norm, the discussion around mental health is not only pivotal but also urgent. It's important to understand the circumstances and factors that influence our mental health in this modern era, and equally critical to identify and implement effective strategies for managing and improving it.

5.1. Understanding Mental Health in a Contemporary World

The World Health Organization (WHO) defines mental health as a state of well-being in which an individual realizes their own abilities, can cope with the normal stresses of life, can work productively and effectively, and is able to contribute to their community. This definition brings attention to several aspects of the human experience that relate to mental health, thereby making it clear that mental health cannot be viewed in isolation but rather as an integral component of overall wellbeing.

Now, more than ever before, our mental health is being challenged. Factors that were already contributing to mental health issues, such as work stress, the pace and pressure of modern life, and societal expectations, have been exacerbated by recent events. The global COVID-19 pandemic, economic insecurities, political polarities, and the utilitarian lifestyle forced upon by digital technologies are uniquely contemporary challenges that pose a significant threat to our collective mental health.

Mental health disorders such as depression, anxiety, and bipolar disorder are prevalent today. According to WHO, approximately one in four people in the world will be affected by mental or neurological disorders at some point in their lives. This statistic is alarming and serves as a call to action for us to understand and tackle mental health issues.

5.2. The Impact of Modern Lifestyle on Mental Health

The pace of modern life can be both invigorating and overwhelming, with constant deadlines, incessant notifications, and societal pressures. Work-related stress is on the rise, with employees feeling constantly 'on' due to technology's unrelenting reach. The repercussions are substantial, leading to issues such as burnouts, disruptive sleep patterns, emotional disturbances, and lack of time for relaxation or nurturing relationships.

Along with the advent of digital technologies come the perils of social media. There is a body of research linking excessive social media usage with negative impacts on mental health. Comparing oneself with others, cyberbullying, lack of genuine interpersonal interactions, reduced physical activity leading to unhealthy lifestyles, and, in extreme cases, addiction to the internet, are all potential hazards that relate to digital technologies.

5.3. Economic Stressors and Mental Health

Financial stress is another vital factor affecting mental health in modern times. The pressure to earn a decent living, the fear of job loss, income inequality, and economic recessions lead to stress, anxiety, and depression. Economic insecurity directly impacts an individual's sense of self-worth, leading to low self-esteem and mental health disorders.

The COVID-19 pandemic has further compounded these economic stressors. Job loss, salary cuts, small business failures, and increased household debts have triggered a mental health crisis that the world was ill-prepared to handle.

5.4. The Political Climate and Mental Health

The political climate also plays a significant role in mental health. Persistent political polarization, civil unrest, and uncertain futures are sources of chronic stress. People are increasingly experiencing a phenomenon known as 'headline stress disorder', caused by the endless cycle of unsettling news. This negatively impacts an individual's mental health by creating feelings of fear, anxiety, and helplessness.

5.5. The Promise of Stoicism in Modern Mental Health Contexts

As we navigate this ocean of uncertainty, the ancient philosophy of Stoicism provides a beacon of hope. It encourages us to focus our energies on what we control, embrace life's vicissitudes, and cultivate inner peace despite external situations. Its principles are deeply rooted in notions of Acceptance, Wisdom, Courage, and Moderation, which resonate with modern concepts of positive psychology and cognitive-behavioral therapy.

Applying Stoic practices can help modern individuals deal with the relentless pressures of contemporary life, find meaning, take mindful actions, and build resilience. By teaching us to distinguish between what lies in our control and what does not, Stoicism empowers us to not be unnerved by external happenings, thereby promoting mental equilibrium.

As we conclude this chapter, remember that the journey to mental heal this is not a linear one. It's about understanding, accepting, and continually working to improve, with the knowledge that there is always room for progress and growth. Despite the challenges of the modern world, mental wellbeing is attainable and closer than it may often seem by adopting practices such as Stoicism. In the chapters to follow, we delve deeper into Stoicism's core principles to pave the way to improved mental health.

Chapter 6. Stoic Strategies for Coping with Stress and Anxiety

In order to begin exploring stoic strategies for coping with stress and anxiety, one must first establish a strong foundational understanding of stoic philosophy. Often, stoicism is mistakenly conflated with indifference or lack of emotion. However, this couldn't be further from the truth. On the contrary, stoicism is a potent tool for emotional regulation and resilience in the face of adversity.

6.1. The Stoic Perspective

Stoicism revolves around the idea that while we may not have control over external circumstances, we have complete control over our thoughts and actions. This fundamental principle underpins all stoic philosophies and strategies. In the context of stress and anxiety, the stoics would suggest altering our perspective towards the stressor rather than trying to replace it.

For instance, when facing a challenging situation, we often have a habitual response of viewing it as inconvenient or stressful. The stoics would advise viewing this situation as an opportunity to grow or learn something instead. This change in perception can drastically alleviate feelings of stress and anxiety, as we begin to frame our experiences positively rather than negatively.

6.2. Negative Visualization

Imagine for a moment, waking up one morning to find that all your material possessions are gone. Your house, car, and all other tangible belongings have disappeared. How would you feel? Probably shocked, anxious, and upset.

But now, imagine after picturing this scenario, you open your eyes and realize it was merely a thought experiment. All your possessions are right where they left them. Suddenly, you might feel an overwhelming sense of gratitude. This exercise is a classic Stoic practice known as 'negative visualization'.

Negative visualization trains our brains to appreciate what we have rather than constantly yearning for more. By occasionally imagining worst-case scenarios and realizing they are not our reality, we can dramatically increase our contentment and reduce anxiety and stress.

6.3. Dichotomy of Control

Many instances of stress and anxiety arise from our futile attempts to control the uncontrollable. Stoic philosophy advocates for understanding the "dichotomy of control," the distinction between things within our control – our own actions and thoughts - and things outside it, such as the actions and thoughts of others, or random events.

Once we internalize this grasp of control, we can focus on controlling our reactions. If a negative event occurs, rather than wallowing in stress or anxiety, we can choose how we respond. Reclaiming this power over our personal reactions is profoundly liberating and an effective way to mitigate stress and anxiety.

6.4. Practicing Dispassion

Another key Stoic strategy is practicing dispassion or viewing situations objectively. Dispassion doesn't mean becoming emotionless, but rather removing the emotional bias from our perceptions so we can see events for what they are, not what we feel about them.

By observing our feelings of stress or anxiety without judgment, we can understand them and accept them for what they are – just feelings. This act of conscious separation from our emotions enables us to gain insights into our triggers and modulate our responses more effectively, reducing the hold stress and anxiety have on us.

6.5. Stoic Meditation

Stoicism also espouses a form of meditation focused on mindfulness and reflection. Stoic meditation is a tool for grounding oneself in the present moment and cultivating an objective understanding of our thoughts and anxieties. Taking time to relax, breathe, and objectively examine the sources of our stress helps shift our focus from the overwhelming emotion to actionable solutions.

6.6. Preparing for Adversity

Preparation is a crucial aspect of Stoicism, especially when it comes to dealing with stressful situations. Stoics believe that by contemplating adversity, which means thinking about how things could go wrong, and preparing for it mentally in advance can help in minimizing its impact and reducing anxiety.

In conclusion, the Stoic approach to managing stress and anxiety revolves around the control we have over our thoughts and actions, the practice of negative visualization, understanding of the dichotomy of control, practicing dispassion, meditation, and preparation for adversity. These strategies provide us with a solid foundation to react to stress and anxiety more effectively, fostering resilience and inner peace in the process.

Chapter 7. The Stoic's Path to Self-Acceptance

Understanding ourselves is the first step in the journey to self-acceptance. Acceptance of oneself is a transformative process that allows for the blossoming of mental tranquility, something that the Stoics held at high regard. The cornerstone of our self-acceptance lies in understanding that we are not perfect and acknowledging our fallibility.

7.1. Recognizing Your Fallibility

As humans, we are susceptible to errors, misjudgments, and emotional upheavals. Stoic philosophers understood this inherent fallibility of our species. Seneca once wisely stated, "Errare humanum est, sed perseverare diabolicum" (To err is human, but to persist is diabolical). Recognizing our fallibility not only sensitizes us towards our imperfections but also makes us more forgiving towards others. We realize that, like us, they too are imperfect beings, prone to mistakes.

7.2. Accepting Imperfections

Acceptance, according to the Stoics, is the response to our acknowledged fallibility. By accepting our imperfections, we unchain ourselves from the weights of unnecessary self-loathing and guilt. Epictetus said, "It's not what happens to you, but how you react to it that matters." Hence, the acceptance of our imperfections is not an approval of mediocrity, but a call to act towards improvement without self-burdening grief.

7.3. Understanding Control

The Stoics espoused the concept of separable control, dividing life events into things we control and things we don't. Epictetus illustrated this through the metaphor of the archer: "The archer's goal is to hit the target. However, once the arrow has left his hands, it is beyond his control." It is a call for us to do our best in areas within our control and accept the outcomes that aren't.

7.4. Creating an Internal Moral Compass

Stoicism is a philosophy grounded on virtue. Your internal moral compass, therefore, must be steadfast and unwavering by external influences. It should guide your thoughts, actions, and reactions. Marcus Aurelius, a Roman Emperor and the last of the Five Good Emperors, was a stoic philosopher who understood the importance of a strong moral compass. According to him, "Anything in any way beautiful derives its beauty from itself and asks nothing beyond itself." Practice living with integrity and sincerity, reflecting on your actions, and continually striving to rectify your moral failings. A reliable moral compass, cemented by your virtues, makes self-acceptance effortless and rewards you with a sense of fulfillment.

7.5. Dealing with Negative Emotions

Negative emotions, if unchecked, can obstruct the path of self-acceptance. Feelings of jealousy, anger, and resentment erode our self-esteem and engender a sense of unworthiness. The Stoics advise us to question and rationalize every negative emotion. Does the feeling of annoyance increase your worth or aid in your growth? Certainly not! Plotinus, a follower of Stoicism, said, "Withdraw into yourself and look. And if you do not find yourself beautiful yet, act as does the creator of a statue."

7.6. Practicing Inner Resilience

Inner resilience is the parting gift of Stoicism's path to self-acceptance. With this, one cultivates an unshakeable poise, an agile mind that can sustain any turmoil life may conspire to throw. Herein lies the advantage of practicing the Stoic principles - they equip us with the fortitude to persist in our journey to self-acceptance, irrespective of the external adversities.

Our life, as posited by the Stoics, is akin to a rough, turbulent sea. The undercurrents threaten to destabilize us, the waves threaten to break us, and the storm threatens to obliterate us. In this vast, tumultuous sea, the wisdom of Stoicism acts as our anchor. Mind you, an anchor does not prevent the storm; it doesn't stop the waves from lashing and the wind from howling. But it gives us the courage to stay put, facing the adversities head-on, all the while firmly holding onto our virtues, our stability, undeterred and unbroken.

Self-acceptance, as we journey through it, is not a destination but a constant process; it is not an act but a habit. It is a quest that demands courage, persistence, and above all, a heart willing to understand and accept oneself.

Having explored in such depth the Stoic's path to self-acceptance, you are now better equipped with the lens of Stoicism. You can now see the world - and yourself - with a more compassionate, nurturing perspective. Hold this perspective close, recall it in times of self-doubt, and use it to guide your thoughts and actions. For you, with your newly acquired wisdom of Stoicism, are your best guide on the path to self-acceptance.

Chapter 8. Applications of Stoicism in Daily Life

Stoicism isn't just a philosophical concept to debate and discuss; it's a practical guide to life that can be applied each and every day. In essence, stoicism teaches us to detach from things we cannot control so that we may live with tranquility and joy in the face of whatever life throws at us. This chapter will carefully guide readers through the numerous practical applications of stoicism in daily life.

8.1. Starting the Day with Stoicism

A stoic approach to life begins as soon as you open your eyes each morning. Instead of rushing into the day, take a few mindful moments to reflect on the wisdom of renowned Stoic philosophers.

Marcus Aurelius, a Roman emperor and renowned Stoic, habitually reminded himself each morning that he was likely to encounter difficult people - but it was his response to them that he could control, not their actions. It's a powerful mindset to start the day: recognizing that challenges will inevitably arise, but reinforcing your power to choose your response.

8.2. Learning to Differentiate Between What You Can and Can't Control

One of the fundamental tenets of Stoic philosophy is understanding the difference between what you can and cannot control. Marcus Aurelius aptly put it: "You have power over your mind - not outside events. Realize this, and you will find strength."

Internalizing this lesson is both liberating and empowering. It eases unnecessary anxiety and encourages more effective problem-solving by focusing on actionable aspects of situations.

In practice, train your mind to differentiate external events (such as weather, traffic, or someone else's mood) from internal matters under your control (like your reactions, judgments, and actions). Commit to expending energy only on the latter, thereby leading to a more peaceful and productive state of being.

8.3. Responding to Negative Emotions with Stoic Strength

Negative emotions are often generated by our response to perceived adverse situations. Stoicism, however, teaches us that these are not intrinsically bad situations but judgments that our mind make about reality.

Understanding that emotions are largely a result of our own judgements can greatly change the way we manage negativity. Instead of giving in to these feelings, acknowledging them as self-created allows us to reassess and change our judgments, using reason and logic to align them more closely with reality.

8.4. Practicing Gratitude and Appreciating the Present Moment

Stoicism encourages a sense of appreciative joy for the present moment. Epictetus, another well-regarded Stoic philosopher, proposed that we should "make the best use of what is in our power and take the rest as it happens."

Instead of dwelling on past regrets or dreading the future, extract joy from the present moment. Integrate small practices into your daily routine to help foster this mindset. A simple exercise is jotting down three things each day that you're grateful for. This habit not only makes you more mindful but also helps nurture a positive outlook on life.

8.5. Embracing Mortality for a More Fulfilled Life

Stoicism advised practicing memento mori – the reflection on one's mortality. Though it might feel morbid, remembering that life is fleeting encourages us to see each moment's inherent worth and act with kindness, integrity, and courage.

8.6. Conclusion: The Daily Integration of Stoic Philosophy

Bringing stoicism into everyday life is a process, not a one-time event. It requires active reflection, continual learning and consistent practice. By striving to control only what's in your power and acknowledging the transient nature of life and events, you can nurture a more resilient, tranquil and fulfilling existence. Over time, these principles can form a sturdy foundation for your mental well-being, leading to a healthier, more peaceful, and purposeful life.

The next chapter will dive deeper into more sophisticated Stoic practices and principles, arming you with additional tools to enhance resilience and inner peace.

Stoicism isn't a quick-fix but a lifelong journey. Yet, it's a journey worth embarking on, for it has the potential to fundamentally change the way we perceive and respond to the world, creating a balanced, resilient you at peace with your inner self and the world around you.

Chapter 9. Case Studies: Stoicism in Practice

In this chapter, we will delve into the real-life instances where stoicism has been applied effectively, illuminating the power of this exceptional philosophy in practical circumstances. Through these case studies, we aim to provide a significant insight into the utility of stoic principles when it comes to enhancing mental health, and to equip readers with the necessary tools to apply these tenets in their own lives.

9.1. Case Study 1: Overcoming Fear and Anxiety

Our first case revolves around a noteworthy personality - John, a renowned entrepreneur. He raised his startup from the ground with sheer dedication and hard-work. But with constant pressure and looming uncertainties, John found himself grappling with intense anxiety. Despite his successes, he often found himself crippled with fear of future hurdles. This is where Stoic philosophy served as a beacon of hope.

John started imbibing the principles of Stoicism into his daily routine. One significant concept he practiced was 'Amor Fati' - the love of one's fate. John realized that fear of the unseen future, essentially things not under his control, was fueling his anxiety. By accepting his fate enthusiastically and understanding that one only has control over responses and actions, he began to experience a drastic reduction in his anxiety levels.

9.2. Case Study 2: Resilience in the Face of Adversity

Angela, a survivor of a catastrophic accident, forms our second case study. The mishap not only caused her physical trauma but also left her reeling with mental despair. Life, for her, seemed an arduous journey of constant struggle.

When introduced to Stoicism, Angela received the strength she needed. The Stoic emphasis on the dichotomy of control became her guiding principle. She understood that while she couldn't control the accident that happened to her, she did have control over how she responded to it, to her recovery.

This empowering shift in perspective spurred her rehabilitation journey and helped Angela cultivate a profound resilience against adversity.

9.3. Case Study 3: Cultivating Serenity in Turbulent Times

Consider the case of Michael, a manager at a multinational firm. His hectic job, filled with relentless deadlines and high stakes, was a constant source of stress. This stress began to take a toll on his mental well-being and interpersonal relationships.

However, the Stoic exercises of 'Negative Visualization' and 'Meditation on Mortality' played a transformative role in Michael's life. The former approach compelled him to consider the worst possible outcomes of situations, which allowed him to appreciate what he had. The latter acted as a reminder of the impermanence of everything - problems, life, and stress itself.

These exercises enabled Michael to anchor his mental peace amidst turbulence, thereby enhancing his overall quality of life.

9.4. Case Study 4: Harnessing Stoicism for Emotional Regulation

The last case study focuses on Sarah, a college student who often struggled with intense bouts of emotion. From seething anger to overwhelming sadness, her emotions were highly volatile.

Stoicism, specifically, the concept of 'View from Above', provided her with the emotional regulation she needed. By using the technique to shift her perspective, observing her circumstances as a small fragment of a vast cosmos, Sarah began seeing her emotional upheavals in a more distanced and less personally affecting manner.

By applying Stoic Philosophy, Sarah developed the ability to regulate her emotions wisely, promoting a healthy mental state amidst the tumultuous college life.

9.5. Conclusion

These four real-life examples provide a concise, yet impactful illustration of stoicism's efficacy. By understanding and implementing these strategies, each individual empowered themselves to conquer their unique mental hurdles. As showcased, the timeless wisdom of stoicism can serve as an enriching tool to navigate through life's hardships, paving the way towards a more balanced mental state and a tranquil life.

Chapter 10. Bridging the Gap: Stoicism and Modern Psychiatry

The popularity of Stoicism, a school of philosophy ascended in the 3rd century BC, has experienced a significant resurgence in the 21st century. Often seen as an ideal philosophy for challenging times, it provides tools and strategies to cultivate the virtues of wisdom, courage, justice, and temperance. Despite its antiquity, Stoicism's core principles have incredible relevance within the realms of modern psychiatry, playing an instrumental role in building resilience and fostering emotional wellness.

10.1. Stoicism: A Primer

Epictetus, a significant contributor to Stoic thought, declared: "We are disturbed not by things, but by the views which we take of them." This simple yet profound statement encapsulates the heart of Stoic philosophy—an emphasis on managing our reactions and perceptions instead of trying to control external circumstances.

Stoicism supports our priorities' clarification, allowing us to focus on what we can directly influence—our attitudes, beliefs, and reactions—and accept what we cannot. It encourages mindfulness, discipline, and thoughtful action, often utilizing reflection and introspection as central tools. Importantly, it does not advocate for repression or denial of emotions but rather teaches us how to handle them in healthier ways.

10.2. Modern Psychiatry: Contemporary Approaches to Mental Health

Modern psychiatry is a multifaceted field encompassing various approaches and interventions, aiming to alleviate mental health concerns. Techniques vary widely, from cognitive-behavioral therapies designed to reconfigure negative thought patterns, psychodynamic therapy focusing on unconscious thoughts and perceptions, pharmacological interventions, mindfulness practices, and more.

The goal of modern psychiatry is not only symptom reduction but also seeks to foster resilience, improve quality of life, and nurture long-term psychological well-being. It encourages an understanding of the interconnectedness between our thoughts, emotions, behavior, and life experiences.

10.3. The Interface of Stoicism and Psychiatry

In understanding the points of intersection between Stoicism and modern psychiatry, it is beneficial to recognize their shared goals—nurturing resilience, self-control, and emotional wellness. Both encourage individuals to become aware of their internal experiences and patterns of thought, prompting a recognized 'paradigm shift' in perspective.

Cognitive-Behavioral Therapy (CBT), one of the pivotal therapeutic approaches in modern mental health, is deeply rooted within Stoic philosophy. CBT focuses on the role of cognition (thoughts) in the way we feel and act. By transforming maladaptive thought patterns, it aims to influence emotions and behaviors positively. It resonates strongly with the original Stoic teaching illuminating the value of controlling our reactions to external circumstances.

Humanistic approaches within psychiatry, emphasizing the individual's self-determination, personal growth, and the importance of present-focused mindfulness, share a profound commonality with Stoicism. Both approaches underline the significance of taking responsibility for our actions and promote the cultivation of virtues for lifelong well-being.

Mindfulness, both as a standalone practice and an integral part of several therapeutical approaches, encourages present-focused, non-judgmental awareness—a concept that aligns wonderfully with the Stoic emphasis on self-awareness and acceptance.

10.4. Stoicism in Clinical Practice

Within the realm of clinical practice, the integration of Stoic principles can offer a supportive framework for clients as they navigate therapy. Through guided reflection and introspection, led by a trained professional, clients can utilize Stoic principles to manage life's volatility better, finding stability within themselves even amidst external change and disorder.

Stoic elements can be found explicitly within Cognitive Behavioral Therapy, Dialectical Behavior Therapy, Rational Emotive Behavior Therapy, and Acceptance and Commitment Therapy, among others. Moreover, Stoicism's core tenets can serve as useful adjuncts to broader therapeutic work, regardless of the chosen methodology.

10.5. Example Exercises For Blending Stoicism and Psychiatry

Several exercises amalgamate stoicism into modern mental health practices effectively. For instance, - Negative Visualization: By periodically anticipating worst-case scenarios (losses or setbacks), we can appreciate what we have in the present and develop resilience in the face of future adversities. - Voluntary Discomfort: Brief, intentional experiences of discomfort (like a cold shower or fasting) help increase our resilience and decrease attachment to comfort. - Mindfulness Practice: Grounding techniques and mindfulness exercises help us engage fully with the present moment and decrease preoccupation with distressing past events or anxious predictions regarding the future.

10.6. Changing Perspectives for Life Transformation

The blending of Stoicism and modern psychiatry offers a potent combination for those seeking a path to inner peace and stability. Notably, while Stoicism gives us a new lens through which to view our experiences, modern psychiatric practices provide us with tangible techniques and interventions to manage our mental and emotional well-being.

The fervor around de-stigmatizing mental health has grown exponentially in recent years, encouraging a broader understanding and acceptance of psychiatric and psychotherapeutic practices. It is in this evolving environment that the wisdom of the Stoic philosophers can truly shine, lending us the resilience and mental fortitude that our circumstances require.

By learning to adjust our responses to the world, cultivate emotional equilibrium, and foster internal resilience, we equip ourselves with essential skills for enduring life's unpredictability. In the face of inevitable changes, setbacks, and challenges, the marriage of Stoicism and psychiatry can truly help us reach an enduring sense of tranquility and become our most resilient selves.

Chapter 11. Treading Forward: Your Personal Journey into Stoicism

To embark on a transformative journey into the heart of Stoicism is to engage in a profound dialog with one's self. Often, we remain obscured to our own thoughts, emotions, and reactions. Stoicism, as a philosophical practice, impels us to turn the gaze inwards. As you tread forward into this rich and intensely personal terrain, remember that each step you take is an assertion of your own power over your life and your emotions.

11.1. Understanding Stoicism

A Greek philosophical school founded by Zeno of Citium in the early 3rd century BCE, Stoicism is a practice of personal ethics informed by its system of logic and its views on the natural world. The Stoic's central tenet is that we don't control and cannot rely on external events, only ourselves and our responses. This very understanding forms the cornerstone of our exploration into Stoicism and its impact on mental health.

11.2. A Rewarding Challenge

Venturing into Stoicism won't necessarily be easy; it demands inner confrontation and introspection, and these can be taxing endeavors. But the rewards are rich - life in accord with virtue, inner peace, resilience, detachment from trivial disturbances, and a profound connection with the universe.

11.3. The Four Cardinal Virtues

Stoicism is built upon four cardinal virtues: wisdom, courage, justice, and temperance. Incorporating these virtues into your daily life is your first stride toward a Stoic way of living.

- Wisdom: Making the best use of knowledge and understanding things as they are without being influenced by personal emotions.

- Courage: Not just physical but moral courage to stand for what is right.

- Justice: To treat all humans with fairness and kindness.

- Temperance: Moderation in all things.

11.4. Embrace Amor Fati

A Latin phrase meaning 'love of fate', Amor Fati is the mindset that you take on for making the best out of anything that happens in your life. Embrace the flow of life, recognize and accept events as they occur.

11.5. Dichotomy of Control: Inside Out

The core principle of Stoicism is the Dichotomy of Control. It's the explicit understanding that some things are within our control while others are not. The key lies in directing our energies to what we can influence and detaching from what we cannot.

11.6. Daily Meditations

Marcus Aurelius, one of the most known Stoic philosophers, wrote a series of personal writings, now known as 'Meditations'. Daily reflection on these teachings can offer a calming and reinforcing agent throughout your journey.

11.7. Dealing with Negative Emotions

Stoicism provides us with the tools to handle our emotions more effectively. When you find yourself swept away by the tide of anger, anxiety, or sadness, Stoicism can act as an anchor, lending a sense of stability amidst the storm.

11.8. Practicing Stoic Exercises

Stoic exercises are designed to help you internalize the principles of the philosophy and integrate them into your daily life. One such exercise is Premeditatio Malorum (the premeditation of evils), a strategy where you imagine things that could go wrong or challenges you might face.

11.9. Stoicism and Mindfulness

Similar to mindfulness, Stoic practices encourage us to be present in the moment, observing our thoughts, emotions without attaching judgment to them. This heightened sense of awareness strengthens our mental reserves and provides a clarity seldom experienced.

11.10. On Simplicity and Minimalistic Living

Stoics believed in a simple and minimalistic life, free from the excesses of human desires. They advocated the reduction of unnecessary worries and material possessions to achieve tranquility.

As our exploration into Stoicism unfolds, remember that this is not an overnight transformation, but a gradual and continuous journey. Embrace the teachings of Stoicism quietly, calmly, and with patience. In every moment of tranquility, every flash of insight, every bout of resilience, know that Stoicism is slowly working its magic within you. Own your journey, for it is a manifestation of your ability to change, to grow, and to flourish.